WEATHER MAKES THEM MOVE

MANATEE MIGRATION

by Rachel Rose

Consultant: Beth Gambro
Reading Specialist, Yorkville, Illinois

Minneapolis, Minnesota

Teaching Tips

Before Reading

- Look at the cover of the book. Discuss the picture and the title.
- Ask readers to brainstorm a list of what they already know about manatees. What can they expect to see in this book?
- Go on a picture walk, looking through the pictures to discuss vocabulary and make predictions about the text.

During Reading

- Read for purpose. Encourage readers to think about manatee movement as they are reading.
- Ask readers to look for the details of the book. Why do manatees migrate?
- If readers encounter an unknown word, ask them to look at the sounds in the word. Then, ask them to look at the rest of the page. Are there any clues to help them understand?

After Reading

- Encourage readers to pick a buddy and reread the book together.
- Ask readers to name a reason manatees move. Find a page that tells about this thing.
- Ask readers to write or draw something they learned about manatee migration.

Credits:
Cover and title page, © 33karen33/iStock; 3, © Andrea Izzotti/iStock; 5, © Greg Amptman/Shutterstock; 7, © 33karen33/iStock; 8–9, © npassmann/iStock; 11, © Thierry Eidenweil/Shutterstock; 13, © gary powell/Shutterstock; 14–15, © Thierry Eidenweil/Shutterstock; 17, © somdul/Shutterstock; 18–19, © Thierry Eidenweil/iStock; 21, © gary powell/Shutterstock; 22T, © Nicolas Larento/Adobe Stock; 22B, © melissa/Adobe Stock; 23TL, © Unwind/Adobe Stock; 23TM, © Mark Winfrey/Shutterstock; 23TR, © davit85/Adobe Stock; 23BL, © solar22/Shutterstock; 23BM, © by-studio/Shutterstock; 23BR, © Tomas Ragina/Shutterstock, © Marian Weyo/Shutterstock.

Library of Congress Cataloging-in-Publication Data

Names: Rose, Rachel, 1968- author.
Title: Manatee migration / by Rachel Rose.
Description: Minneapolis, Minnesota : Bearport Publishing Company, [2024] |
  Series: Weather makes them move | Includes bibliographical references
  and index.
Identifiers: LCCN 2022059200 (print) | LCCN 2022059201 (ebook) | ISBN
  9798888220672 (hardcover) | ISBN 9798888222652 (paperback) | ISBN
  9798888223826 (ebook)
Subjects: LCSH: Manatees--Migration--Juvenile literature. | Manatees--Seasonal distribution--Juvenile literature.
Classification: LCC QL737.S63 R69 2024 (print) | LCC QL737.S63 (ebook) |
  DDC 599.55156/8--dc23/eng/20221215
LC record available at https://lccn.loc.gov/2022059200
LC ebook record available at https://lccn.loc.gov/2022059201

Copyright © 2024 Bearport Publishing Company. All rights reserved. No part of this publication may be reproduced in whole or in part, stored in any retrieval system, or transmitted in any form or by any means, electronic, mechanical, photocopying, recording, or otherwise, without written permission from the publisher.

For more information, write to Bearport Publishing, 5357 Penn Avenue South, Minneapolis, MN 55419.

Contents

Brrr, **it is Cold!** 4

On the Move! 22

Glossary 23

Index 24

Read More 24

Learn More Online 24

About the Author 24

Brrr, it is Cold!

Brrr!

The water is getting cold.

It is time for manatees to move.

But where do they go?

Manatees live in **coastal** waters around the world.

Some are by the shores of the United States.

These are called Florida manatees.

Florida manatees are very big.

But they do not have a lot of **fat** on their bodies.

This makes it easy for them to get cold.

Being in cold water can make these big animals sick.

They can even die if they get too cold.

Manatees need to be where the water is warm.

Warm water is easy to find in the summer.

But then the **season** changes.

Water **temperatures** drop.

It is time to swim to warmer Florida waters.

Manatees usually live by themselves.

But when they travel they may swim with others.

Manatees need **energy** to make this trip.

Luckily, there is lots of food along the way.

They munch on water plants as they go.

Once in Florida, manatees need to stay warm.

Some swim to the warm waters in rivers and **bays**.

Others get together to share their body heat.

When spring comes, the coastal waters warm up.

Manatees can swim home until next winter.

Weather makes them move!

On the Move!

Migration (mye-GRAY-shuhn) is when animals move from one place to another. Often, they travel far. Let's learn more about manatee migration!

Manatees usually swim south in November. They swim back home in April.

They usually swim about 3 miles per hour (5 kph).

Glossary

bays parts of the ocean that are partly surrounded by land

coastal having to do with where land and water meet

energy the power needed by all living things to be active and stay alive

fat something under the skin that helps keep animals warm

season a part of the year marked by its weather

temperatures how hot or cold things are

Index

coastal 6, 20
fat 8
Florida 12, 19
plants 16
season 12
spring 20

Read More

Culliford, Amy. *Manatees (Under the Sea Animals).* Coral Springs, FL: Seahorse Publishing, 2022.

LaPlante, Walter. *Manatees (Ocean Animals).* New York: Gareth Stevens Publishing, 2020.

Learn More Online

1. Go to **www.factsurfer.com** or scan the QR code below.
2. Enter "**Manatee Migration**" into the search box.
3. Click on the cover of this book to see a list of websites.

About the Author

Rachel Rose is a writer who lives in California. She swims in the ocean every day, even when it gets very cold!